Success Is Not Accident

Probably You Need Me As Your Life Coach: Check It Out!

INTRODUCTION

If it has already happened to you to sit down and think about your life and think about different ideas towards making a change in your life and you ended up not doing anything, you might need assistance from a life coach. That lack of taking actions might be due to different things. Therefore, in most cases, that inability to take action is due, mainly, to doubts, confusions, fear, insecurities, negativities that are going on in your mind. If you feel like you want to move on and take action and make a change in your life but you remain stuck, it a sign that you might need to seek some assistance from a life coach. The kind of help you need is offered by a life coach.

A life coach like in sports, is someone who has that capacity to help you by giving you that needed push to get you out from being stuck and so that you can start moving forward. The life coach does not leave you alone in the middle of the journey. S/he stays with you all the way until you reach out to your goals. A life coach will help you to take a move towards the future and not by focusing and looking too much in the past. The reason why the life couch provides their help by not looking into the past is simply because in most cases, the fear, the insecurities that keep you stuck in inactivity find their source in your past. For that reason past is not going to help that much in your new journey given that most of the job to be offered by the life coach is to help you to approach life differently and positively and help you to start a new chapter to start viewing life and the world differently.

Now the question comes up to know if you really need a life coach. It is all up to you to decide if you need a life coach or not. But the reality is that, if you feel you want to move on and make a change in your life and really can't do it or you simply remain in confusion, you should consider seeking assistance from a life coach. You need some help because something is not going well somewhere. If you can do it by yourself that is fine, you don't need any assistance, then move on and do something and stop complaining, stop judging and stop blaming others for your current bad situation. But if you still remain in confusion, doubts lack of confidence, low self esteem then you need some help. You need assistance from a life coach. Don't be shy. Don't hesitate. Shout for assistance. A life coach will be there to help out.

A life coach will help you through empowering you thought your journey of change from the goal setting phase to the achievements of your goals. The life coach will provide you guidance while setting either your personal or professional goals in your life. In other words, a life coach will help you to achieve your life goals through guiding you and motivating you while you are trying to overcome what is making you stuck and keeping you in the same place that you might ignore or you might not be aware of but which still leads you to feel powerless and effortless to take any action and leave your doubts behind you and move on.

CHAPI: WHAT LIFE COACHES DO?

A life coach helps you through providing you the needed mentorship and accompaniment while you are trying to take action towards making a change in your life. A life coach assists you to fix your life's problems that have kept you in hostage and in captivity which are the cause that made you remain stuck in one place for so long. There is a reason why you fail to move on and make a change in your life. You probably need some help. Check it out. A life coach will work with you as a motivator though putting in place a couple of strategies according to your particular need. A life coach will be in your accompanying throughout your journey of change until you reach out to your life goals. In that sense, a life coach is different from a counselor or a consultant. While a consultant might only have to intervene on a very specific and particular area of your life for a given period of time, a life coach intervenes and works with you in all aspects of your life from your thinking and mindset change, works with you while you are setting your goals, stays with you during the execution of your change and will always be there with you to provide you with the needed encouragement, motivation, facilitation and needed accompaniment all the way though in your journey until you achieve your life set goals.

Like in sports, the team coach stays until the match is over to ensure the players are executing the provided instructions and continues to provide needed advice to the players all along the entire match. The same scenario also applies in the life coaching industry. More often, when people are trying to make a difference, they have difficulties to decide about the goals to set as they might lack some needed self-confidence due to their inner insecurity, doubts and fear they might have in their mind. It can also be due simply to lack of awareness of what are their strengths or it can be due to failing to sort out their strengths and weaknesses.

More often, when people are asked a question to talk about their strengths and weaknesses, they don't have enough to say, or they find it difficult to talk about their weaknesses, not because they don't really have strengths and weaknesses, but simply because they are confused when it comes to distinguishing between their strengths and weaknesses. Generally, they might have some weaknesses they don't want to admit as weaknesses or they don't know they are weaknesses.

If when you are asked to talk about your weaknesses, you find it hard or you find it difficult to talk about your weaknesses or simply you don't know what your weaknesses are, then you might need some assistance from a life coach because the fact is if you don't know your weaknesses or simply you don't want to admit your weaknesses you will confuse your weaknesses and your strengths. The truth is, with that confusion you can't go far in your journey towards change. The real change comes from your capacity, to recognize your strengths and your weaknesses, or from admitting your weaknesses and start making some efforts to overcome them in order to be able to move on. If you are still in the denial of your weaknesses or you can't even tell what your weaknesses are, then you need assistance from a life coach before you decide to take action to make a change in your life.

It is the role of the life coach to accompany their clients in finding out what are their strengths and weakness prior to move on to goals setting phase. Sincerely speaking some people need that push in finding out what their life purposes are and in setting goals accordingly to materialize and transitioning their life goals into specific and tangible actions.

Some people need a push to acquire that needed self-confidence to take actions and move forward. Strictly, without this push a big number of people might remain stuck where they are for quite a long time as their fear, doubts and confusion or ignorance tend to have much weight on their willingness power to move on. That is where and when the life coach comes in to help and provides the needed support with regards to their clients' mindset change. Life coaching aims at helping the client to achieve their potential and it is meant to be non-judgmental and life coaching is done through a mutual confidential relationship in order to work out.

The life coaching industry is based on the theory according to which the clients have all the solutions to their problems. What the clients need is simply the courage and needed motivation to lead them to overcome their fear, confusion, insecurities, doubts they may even be ignoring. A life coach works with their clients in their efforts to reprogram their mindsets differently by leaving their troubling past behind them and by reprogramming their mindsets positively to fit and to correspond to their new life style they decided to adopt.

A life coach is just a guide. You, as the client, you are the one to do the big part of the job. The life coach will only play the role of encouraging you, motivating you and will ensure that you remain on track with regards to your goals. In other words, the life coaches are there to encourage you as motivators and facilitators but at the same time while playing their role as motivators and as guides, they also hold you accountable in one way or another throughout you journey.

Therefore, the success comes from the client accepting and willing to make the change from the very beginning. The life coach's responsibility will be to help out the client to come up with the needed strategies as well as helping the client in their mindset reprogramming prior to take the first step in their new journey. The primary job of the life coach is consisting in giving a push to clients to accept or recognize their role and responsibilities in their status and in finding out their strengths prior to get started with their journey of making a change in their lives.

If you believe that people can't change their situation and you don't like feedback about your role and responsibilities in your current life situation, that also constitutes a good reason to seek help from a life coach. Changing your life comes from changing your thinking first. If you are always complaining and blaming others for your situation that is another reason why you should seek life coach's assistance as that way of viewing life needs to be handled before you can think of taking any action towards changing your life.

The client's willingness towards change is the key and very fundamental in life coaching. The life coach's job is to help stimulating the willing clients to make a shift. Life coaches are there to help clients to handle their fear, doubts, confusions, negativities that undermine their willingness to make the desired change they are looking forward to making.

There are a big number of people who hate their jobs or simply don't like the jobs they do. But more often, they find it difficult to make a change or are simply unable to change anything about their professional lives. They feel they want to do something to make a change, but they remain stuck in procrastination. This inaction finds its explanation from a variety of factors but with no doubt the failure to change their situation is mainly due to their insecurity, uncertainty, doubts, confusion as well as the lack of awareness of their strengths and weaknesses.

People in this category might need a life coach to help them out. Dealing with this kind of situation must be challenging sometimes if you keep it to yourself and keep talking to yourself alone in silence and in isolation. Getting some help from a life coach must be of a big help in terms of enhancing or generating your self-confidence and your self-trust in terms of making a step forward towards a change in your life. Not only a life coach can be helpful from the very beginning at the goal setting phase but also will be in your accompany during the execution phase and will still be there until the end when you be reaching out to your life goals.

This is made possible in the sense that the life coach will hold you accountable to some extent while cheering you and motivating you in your journey what will surely help you to keep on track during your journey of implementing your plan and strategies towards your desired change.

Some people give the impression that they don't know what they want while they find themselves doing things they don't believe in or which are in contradiction with their values. If you hate your job, and you are willing to change it, but you remain stuck in inaction, that is probably due to your fear, your anxieties, your inner insecurities, your low self-confidence, your low self-esteem. You really need a push from a life coach. You should consider seeking help from a life coach and stop suffering in silence and stop only talking to yourself in isolation. The life coach will work with you to restore your lost self-confidence to get rid of your fears and insecurities which will help you to move on and take action and stop to do things in contradiction with your values.

Feeling like you want to do something to change your bad or uncomfortable life situation and you really end up not doing it, it shows that, there is a problem of confusion and doubt and lack of trust in yourself. It can also be the lack of awareness of your own strengths and weaknesses. If you fall in this category of people, don't be shy, you need some assistance from the life coach. Please shout for help. You need a push from a life coach in order to move forward.

For sure, you have all the capacity and you have all it takes to make a decision and move forward towards making a change in your life. Why you are not doing it and you remain procrastination and in hostage of your past, in your confusion and in your doubts? This is a good question. It is here, when comes up the role of the life coach to help you to respond properly to this why question by focusing your attention on your positive energies. You need to be given that push that will lead you to make your first step forward in terms of challenging your thinking and reprogramming your mindsets differently.

This is the most important and crucial role of the life coach, mostly, when it comes to making a change in mindset and start viewing life from a different angle. This is the most important role of the life coach and each life coach should have this capacity to challenge, influence and stimulate this shift in mindset towards this needed change.

In reality the person is willing to make a change. But, at the same time, there is also some negative energy, doubts and confusion, uncertainly, lack of confidence and lack of trust going on in their minds which, unfortunately, end up in most cases leading and empowering the negative energy to overshadow the positive energy and thus leading to inaction as a result. What the life coach does is to bring more positive energy that adds up to the clients' existing positive energy that is being neutralized or overshadowed by their negative energy and their negative mindsets within their mind and thus leading to inaction.

The reality is once the person gets that needed push from the life coach and makes the first steps towards the change, s/he overcomes that fear, that insecurity, that confusion and that lack of trust that was undermining his/her willingness to make a change. Once the people overcome that phase, there is little chance that they might come back into the old confusing old fashion thinking.

Therefore, there is still a possibility that people might come back in the old thinking, mainly if things don't go as planned in their new journey and that is exactly why the life coach is needed. The life coach has got the responsibility to keep in accompany with their clients until they achieve their goals. That accompaniment of the life coach is meant to prevent and avoid the client to slide back in the old mindset and old mentality just in case things might not go as planned in their new journey of change. It is on this aspect, where the role of the life coach is different from the role of a counselor or a consultant as highlighted previously.

Much more importantly, the role of the life coach is not simply limited to the simple assistance that will end in helping or motivating their clients to reprogram their mindsets and start seeing things differently, but more significantly, the role of the life coach also consists in the continued accompaniment of their clients until they achieve their goals. This accompaniment is so critical in terms of holding the client accountable in sticking on their defined actions during their journey of change in one way or another.

CHAP II: LIFE COACHING AND EMOTIONAL INTELLIGENCE

One of the most important skills the life coach must have is the emotional intelligence. As the saying goes, if you can't manage your own emotions, you can't manage other people's emotions too. And as a matter of fact, there is a lot of work to be done in terms of emotions management in the life coaching job in general and in terms of helping the clients themselves to acquire necessary emotional intelligence in their journey of change in particular.

But before we can go far in discussing the role of emotional intelligence in the life coaching journey, let's first shed some light on the term "emotional intelligence" itself. Emotional intelligence is the capacity to understand your own emotions and other people's emotions in order to be able to put yourself in their shoes, and in order to be able to manage your own emotions as well as to be able to understand and manage other people's emotions. The whole logic behind is that acquiring the capability to manage and control your own emotions and the capacity to understand and manage other people emotions puts you in a position of not letting the emotions controlling you instead on both side (on the side of life coach and on side of their clients as well). Not having the capacity to control your emotions on both sides, will not facilitate the journey and might end up affecting negatively the outcomes of your journey in the end.

Not only life coaches need to have the required emotional intelligence, although they need it the most as a requirement and a condition of their profession, but mostly their clients need to acquire basic emotional intelligence which is necessary in bringing and keeping happiness in their lives. That being said, happiness which we all aspire to have in our lives with no exception, it has to do a lot with emotional intelligence in general. You cannot be happy until you learn how to manage your own emotions as well as managing other's people emotions. In one way or another, you will have to deal with other people in your daily life. There is no way to avoid it or to escape from it.

During your journey of change, you will have to interact with other people's emotions in one way or another or to some extent at some point in your life. Without being fully equipped with the necessary emotional intelligence, you might end up losing your happiness while interacting with the external world. Although none wants this to happen, therefore, without having the necessary emotional intelligence, you might end up losing your happiness from your daily basis interactions with the external world. With no doubt, we are all emotional beings and we can get fragile by other people's emotions very easily if we don't get prepared on how to manage other people's emotions in advance.

Other people's emotions will come your way in one way or another either you want it or not. Without having the basic emotional intelligence, other people's emotions might end up putting you down and take your happiness away. Let alone your own emotions which might also become a source of unhappiness from failing to understand them and manage them and handle them properly.

That being said, let's come back to our life coaching role and responsibility and talk about the role of emotional intelligence in this entire process of accompanying the client towards making a change in their lives. The clients' lack of emotional management also comes into play to explain the clients' failure to make any change in their lives. Frankly speaking, the lack of confidence, the lack of self-trust, the doubts, the confusion and the insecurities that keep the clients stuck in that kind of lifestyle they hate but still fail to change can find their source and their explanation in the failure of a proper management of their own emotions as well.

Consequently, the life coach, in addition to be able to understand and manage their own emotions during the entire course of their clients' life coaching journey, they will also have to be able to understand and manage appropriately their clients' emotions. Failing to do that might lead to failing to help their clients in their efforts to make their desired change. Depending on each case, the life coaching process consisting primarily in helping the clients in understanding their own emotions if there is a need to do so, before leading and taking the same client to the next level of making a decision to change their mindsets and start seeing things and seeing life differently.

It is so vital for the life coach to ensure that the clients are in peace with themselves before making any step moving forward. Otherwise, neglecting this aspect might lead to a kind of resistance from changing or unnecessarily delaying the change of mindset which is a requirement prior to get started with implementing the real actions towards the change. Letting your emotions controlling you or simply failing to ensure that clients are not being controlled by their emotions will surely have a negative impact on the entire life coaching process.

Failing to control one's emotions goes hand in hand with letting unhappiness feelings taking place and taking the lead in one's mind. Unhappy people will be reluctant to make the right and mature decisions towards the change. The mismanagement of painful feelings, for instance, might keep their clients in their previous state of insecurity which is not conducive to a positive change of mindset.

The life coaching industry is based on this theory that the individual is the only one who has all what it takes to make that desired change. The role of the life coach is just to offer guidance and to play his/her role as a motivator and facilitator. That being said, the life coach should keep in mind that there is always a correlation between the client's capacity to change their mindsets and make a change in their life and their emotional intelligence level.

Being able to manage one's emotions goes hand in hand with one's increased self-confidence which is a catalyst that will drive the entire journey of change the client is willing to make. That being said, for the life coach to address the lack of confidence in the client's mind, s/he has to start from ensuring that the clients are being able to understand their own emotions as well as being able to control their emotions and not being controlled by their emotions instead. This is a very important aspect in the life coaching which the life coach will have to handle appropriately before moving forward to the next steps.

It is easy to lead the clients to start taking ownership of their own emotions. All the life coach has to do is to ensure that the clients are in peace with themselves by ensuring that they understand very well their primary responsibility on every aspect of the journey including bringing happiness in their lives. It is as simple as that. It is so important that the clients recognize that, if they are waiting for other people to bring happiness in their lives, they might end up waiting for so long. It is their full responsibility to create that happiness they want and protect it from being taken away under no circumstance. It is only them who can bring that happiness they want into their lives and none else will do it in their place.

Accordingly, based on that awareness, if it happens that someone from outside is trying to take their happiness away they should be able to not allow it. They should put in place a couple of strategies to protect their happiness and avoid their happiness to be taken away by whichever means. Leading the clients to control their emotions can simply be understood that way. Without going into much details, being able to manage your emotions can partly consist in the people's capacity of not allowing themselves to be taken in captivity by undesirable emotions and to be able to let painful feelings or unhappiness go and get out of their mind if they happen to occur for one reason or another.

Leading clients to acquire the basic emotional intelligence can simply consist in telling or teach clients that if it happens that they get shocked, or get hurt or if they happen to get painful feelings, the principle is very simple. They should let that bad feeling, that bad sentiment that bad emotion go immediately. That undesirable emotion has to leave their mind with immediate effect. It is all about avoiding or not to allowing any room for any negativity or any negative energy, or any painful feeling into your mind. As soon as it comes in, you should show it the exit door right away. It is very simple. It all takes is the client's willingness and a couple of efforts.

Clients should be advised that doing that is so beneficial to clients themselves more that it is for anyone else. By doing so, they are actually giving a gift to themselves while doing all it takes to protect and preserve their happiness. Happiness is the ultimate goal of our existence. Everyone wants to live a happy life. We all want to live happily. Happiness should be the only emotion that should be allowed to take the lead and ownership in our lives.

Through bringing clients to recognize their responsibilities in creating and protecting their own happiness, it will become easier for them to preserve their happiness. They will also feel the obligation to protect their happiness all the time, as they need it as a catalyst to move on in their journey of change. Consequently, the client will stop complaining and will stop blaming others for their bad situations and for their own problems.

This change of attitude from the clients' side is highly needed, not only, in terms of understanding and managing their own emotions, but also, this change of attitude is highly needed in the broad sense of changing their mindsets which will surely lead to the client's desired change.

Therefore, it is the role and responsibility of the life coach during the life coaching to ensure that all these elements are put in consideration and all these requirements are met and put in place as they are fundamentals to set and shape the way for the desired change.

CHAP III: ROLE OF EMOTIONAL INTELLIGENCE IN LIFE COACHING

It wouldn't make any sense for clients to seek to make changes in their lives and to seek help from life coaches if their end goal is not to bring more happiness in their lives. The reality is if people are not being able to make any change in their lives while willing do so, they are not being happy people whatsoever.

As I pointed out in the previous chapter, people's failure to take action and move on and make a change in their lives is partly due to anxieties, insecurities, doubts, lack of confidence, confusion and negativity, negative energies that are popping up into their minds. These are symptoms, of not being happy or symptoms of lack of happiness in their minds as well. Happiness does not cohabitate with the state of mind full of insecurities, anxieties, doubts, lack of self-confidence, confusion and negativity and negative energies and negative mindsets.

That being said, the reality is that any attempt leading people to willing to make a change in their lives, comes not only from willing to achieving personal success or professional growth, but also it comes from willing to achieve more self-accomplishment and consequently bringing more quality of life into their lives.

It wouldn't make any sense for people willing to make any change in their lives if the end goal is not to bring more quality of life into their lives. The quality of life which I would like to define here as being the general well-being of individuals or simply the level of happiness in people's lives, is the ultimate goal of all our human activities. We all want and aspire to live happily and bring more quality of life as much as we can into our lives. Subsequently, that being said, people's willing to make any change in their lives, although, it might appear as people are trying to make some transformations in their lives on the financial aspect or professional growth aspect, in most cases, it also has that hidden dimension of bringing or increasing more happiness into their lives as well.

The clients' goals might come and appear in a form of willing to transform, mainly, their financial situations in most of the cases, in form of professional growth or entrepreneurship accomplishment. Therefore, lie coach should keep in mind that this is just a starting point. The main goal of their clients is far away from that. All they are looking for is happiness, and bringing more quality of life into their lives. But in their own views, the way to achieve what they want is to pass through the goals they just set. The financial freedom/independence or the professional growth, set by your clients as their goals are just vehicles, they think in their perceptions will lead them to their hidden desire of more quality of life and more happiness into their lives.

Bringing more quality of life or simply bringing more happiness in people's lives is the ultimate goal or simply it is the goal number one although not stated. Clients might perceive the financial freedom or financial independence or merely the professional growth as the way of achieving more quality of life into their lives. That is fine to let them state their goals that way and the way the wish. But as a life coach you have to keep in mind that, their main goal is to achieve more quality of life into their lives.

Therefore, as we might be aware, more often, achieving the financial freedom or financial independence or professional growth does not always guarantee the quality of life or more happiness into somebody's life. Having this in mind, the life coach should come up with a strategy of accompanying their clients in achieving their stated goals by also focusing on putting in place additional strategies to help their clients achieving the quality of life or bring more happiness into their lives whichever the outcomes of the stated goals might be. This will be a very beneficial strategy that will end up helping clients to also achieve their non-stated "quality of life" goal concurrently.

Accordingly, bringing more happiness into people's lives is a very important aspect of the life coaching and is, in most cases, the ultimate goal, or the main intent of the desired change, although it might not be stated, that pushes clients to willing to make a change in their lives and as a consequence to seek assistance from a life coach as well. For that reason, life coach have to have this in mind and always take it into consideration, although the client might not state it or point it out as being their primary goal or primary intent of seeking your assistance.

As a matter of fact, as a result of what is highlighted above I would define happiness as being people's capacity of being able to satisfy their basic life needs or physiological needs as well as their capacity of being able to make peace with themselves. In other words, happiness is, in addition to be the satisfaction of the life basic needs, it is people's capacity of being able to understand and control not only their emotions but also being able to understand and manage other people's emotions. Understanding other people's emotions mean that people are being able to put themselves in other people's shoes. This is the skill known as the emotional intelligence. That being said happiness would simply be defined, in this context, as a combination of having the capacity to satisfy the basic life needs (physiological needs) as well as having the basic emotional intelligence (capacity to understand and to control their own and other people's emotions).

So, with regards to life coaching, a life coach has to be able to include this emotional skill aspect into the life coaching activities all the way from the beginning of the client's journey towards the achievement of the goals or change their clients want to make in their lives. No assumption should be made about it as it constitutes a very important aspect and surely it is always the ultimate goal of any change clients might want to make in their lives. This is always the main intent behind the clients' willingness to make a change into their lives and which also led the clients to seek assistance from the life coach as well.

As mentioned previously, a life coach should not make any assumption around the happiness aspect in the life couching. As I pointed out in the previous chapters, although clients might not state it clearly, bringing or increasing more happiness into their live is the primary goal of their willingness to make changes into their lives. It is always the end goal of the entire life coaching process. Failing to include the happiness aspect in the equation as well as the client's emotional intelligence aspect might end up unnecessarily delaying the entire process of life coaching and the achievement of the desired change.

That being said not only the life coach has to possess the needed emotional intelligence but also the client's emotional intelligence has to be taken into account from the very beginning of life coaching, during the journey and even at the end and will be highly needed by the client even after achieving the goal set. The emotional intelligence is the foundation that will streamline the life coaching and which will give a push to the desired change. Similarly, it will still be the fundamental element that the client will continue to need to sustain the achieved happiness once the entire change will be achieved.

One more important aspect of the life couching theory is that, in addition to focusing on the future and leave the past behind, in life couching, we believe that and we theorize that it is the client who has to make the change happen and not the life coach or any other external factor. The life couch is just a guide, a facilitator, a motivator, an accompagnateur in the life coaching process. The big part and the big job will be done by the clients themselves. That is why the life coach has to ensure that their clients are fully equipped in all sensitive aspects that require attitudinal change prior to get started with the change itself that their clients want to make in their lives.

In summary to shade more light on this, the role of the life coach should start from helping the clients to acquire the necessary emotional intelligence that they surely need in making a shift in their mindsets and start taking actions towards the desired change they want to see taking place in their lives. Much more importantly, the clients not only need the emotional intelligence during the goal setting phase and in the execution of their desired change but also and more importantly, they will still need emotional intelligence even after achieving the desired change to maintain and sustain their happiness and quality of life.

Bringing more quality of life is always the ultimate goal of everything we do in life. Likewise it is the ultimate goal of any change we might all dream of making into our lives. Life coaches have to know this and always have to take it into account whatever the goals of their clients should be. Any intent to make a change aims at bringing or increasing more quality of life or more happiness into one's life. Although, clients' goals to make a change in their lives might appear to be money oriented or financial freedom or professional growth oriented, life coach has to know that this is just their clients' perceived path to reach out to happiness. That is what they think will help to bring happiness or increase more quality of life into their lives.

CHAP IV: WHERE DOES PEOPLE'S LOW SELF-ESTEEM COME FROM?

There might be so many factors that come into play to explain why people might struggle to make a change in their lives. However, people who are willing to move on and remain stuck and fail to take action, not only their minds are full of confusion, doubts, insecurities, but also their self esteem, their-self confidence and their dignity can also be questionable. One of the responsibilities of a life coach is also to explore the restoration of these three dimensions as well.

As a consequence, clients won't be able to make significant progress with low self-esteem, low self-confidence and low dignity. In most cases people became victims of low self-esteem, low self-confidence as well as low self-dignity from the environment in which they leave or form the type of education they got. Partly, people are not responsible for that lack of self-esteem, that lack of self-confidence and that lack of dignity that make them stuck in the complete inaction, while they are really willing to make a change. It is extremely important for a life coach to pay attention to these three states of mind dimensions in the life coaching as well.

In one of my e-book entitled "**Why some people are rich and other are poor?" Is financial freedom a dream or a reality?** I discuss broadly this aspect where I ask the question of who determines how and what we think. I discussed broadly in this e-book about some research that pointed out that when the child is born, at one hour old, the only program s/he has in her/his brain are only the four genetic codes which are: eat, reproduce, fight, and if it does not work run away. Her/his brain is neutral at birth. Her brain doesn't know what is right and what is wrong. The notion of right and wrong is something we program in our kids after they are born. The child has no low self-esteem, no low self-confidence and no confusion going on in his/her mind.

In this perspective, we can now tell who determines and who decides what we think, the way we think and how we view life and the world when we become adults. With no doubt, our children are with no doubt a replication or a reproduction of their parents and become a duplication of the environment surrounding them. But mainly, they are much more importantly a duplication of their parents from having been in their hands for a very long time and at a critical time of their lives when their brains were so soft and neutral.

That being said, to respond to the question I asked above of who determines what and how we think, it becomes simple. What the children become after birth depends on the environment that surrounds them and depends on how their parents program their brains and mindsets. If children happen to be in good hands, they will be fed with a positive thinking and positive messages and will inherit positive mindsets.

If children are fed with positive messages, they will surely end up endorsing positive mindsets that go hand in hand with a high self-esteem, high self-confidence and will feel a high dignity and valuable in the society. The opposite is also true. In the other way around, when children are fed with negative messages, with lots of negativities, from growing up in hands of parents with low self-esteem, low-self confidence and low self-dignity, that is unfortunately what their parents will be transmitting to them or that is what their parents will be, unintentionally, programming in their brains.

In this same e-book, I broadly discussed how parents constitute the primary influencer of how children think and of how they view life and the world in which they live when they grow up and become adults. Most of the time, unfortunately, parents will be transmitting negative message instead of positive messages. Research pointed out that parents feed at least 23 negative messages to their kids every day.

For the first 18 years of life, while in hands of their parents, kids will be fed with at least 148,000 negative messages. We can see from this illustration to what extent children can become victims of negative mindsets, low self-esteem, low self-confidence and low dignity. Just from inhering this kind of negative mindsets from their parents.

This being said, a life coach has a got a big responsibility to look into these three fundamental state of mind dimensions to determine where their clients stand and if there is a need to get their mindsets reprogrammed differently to correspond and fit the new positive mindsets framework conducive to the new change their clients are trying to make in their lives.

The low self-esteem, the low self-confidence, the low dignity, all those negative messages can tremendously contribute negatively and can lead people or keep them within that feeling of inferiority complex for so long if they are not addressed properly. Fortunately, the good news is that, this can be reversed; the brain can be reprogrammed differently through personal efforts and assistance from professional such as life coaches.

What all these victims need is to be fed with a different and positive messages and that is exactly what the life coach is there to do. It might take so long to change that software and it is understandable. If people were fed with negative messages and were victims of inheriting negative mindsets for decades, it might take time to reverse the software. It is not obvious to expect the same people to reprogram their mindsets overnight. This is mostly what the life coach is there to do during life coaching and that is exactly why life coaching is far away to be an overnight job.

For a life coach, each case, and each client is unique as we are all unique and different from one another. Our uniqueness is due to the fact that we come from different backgrounds and different environments and we have been raised differently as well. No assumption should be made by the life coach. Each and every situation should be handled differently according to the emerging and apparent needs of each and every client.

CONCLUSION
Success is not accident. Success comes from hardworking, self-commitment, self-determination, making the right decisions

which starts from setting our mindsets positively. People who get stuck in inaction might end up complaining and blaming others or blaming the external factors for their uncomfortable and unwanted life situations, but the truth/reality is that the real problem is in their minds instead. In other words, the solution of their problems or the cause of their failure to move on has to be found in their thinking and they can only come from that situation by deciding to change their mindsets and start to think and view the world differently and more importantly in positive manner which is not judgmental.

That is being said, it is here where the role of the life coach comes in to accompany their clients in this entire process of change by making the entire process of change smooth through providing the needed moral and emotional support to their clients. People in this situation really need a push and some motivation. Therefore, this motivation is meant to be provided by a professional, in this case, a life coach, who knows and who understands better the transition these people are going through.

They need accompaniment of a professional who is the life coach in this case. They need a life coach who understands better where they are coming from and where they are heading to. They need a life coach who has a better knowledge of what was keeping them stuck and who knows what it takes to shift from their previous type of thinking to another type of thinking. They need a life coach who understands why they looking for in their new journey and what type of assistance they really need in that process of change. What all these people need is nothing else that encouragements, facilitation and motivation from someone who really understands the problems they were facing and what efforts it might take them to make their desired change.

When people get stuck in inaction and fail to move forward while willing to make a change in their lives, it is a sign that they might need some assistance to some extent form a life coach. Therefore, as highlighted in this book, the role of a life coach is limited. The role of the life coach will only be limited to being just a guide, a motivator, a facilitator and an accompagnateur. The main responsibility to make the change happen is from the clients themselves. On one hand, the life coach on their side, they have to be knowledgeable in general human psychology and have to have extensive emotional intelligence to be able to handle the job that will be awaiting them during this entire journey of change.

Life coach will have to keep in mind that each client is a unique case in itself and should be handled differently and in its specific uniqueness. On the other hand, the life coaching is meant to provide guidance to people who are willing to move on and make a change in their lives but remain confused and remain in doubts and end up failing to take any action. The life coach's assistance will mainly consist of bringing their clients to become aware of their strengths and potentials that are being overshadowed by their negative mindsets and thinking until then.

As far as the life coaches are concerned, their main job is to help the client to get out of their low self-esteem and low self-confidence in order to move on and take needed action to start making a change in their lives. With regards to life coaching profession, in addition to have enough emotional intelligence as pointed out, in order to be able to help their clients efficiently through understanding their emotions and by putting themselves in their clients' shoes, they will also have to ensure that their clients have the basic emotional intelligence that is also a requirement on the clients' side to be able to overcome their confusion, their fear and their doubts in order to move on towards their desired change in a very sustainable manner.

Let me conclude my book on this statement. If you feel that you are willing and trying to make a change in your life, but you end up not doing anything and you remain stuck in inaction and procrastination that is a sign that you need some assistance from a life coach. Don't hesitate and don't be shy, please ask for assistance from a life coach. Life coaches are there to help you out to get out from that situation. The only way you can get yourself out of that unwanted situation is to stop talking to yourself alone in isolation which can only keep you in that same low self-esteem, low self-confidence, doubt and confusion that have been keeping you stuck in one place. You need to admit that you have a problem and ask for help from a life coach. There are so many life coaches out there who can help you out, but if you feel you would like to get some assistance from me particularly, I can be reached out on my following personal email: hakizamungu.massudii@gmail.com

www.ingramcontent.com/pod-product-compliance
Lightning Source LLC
Chambersburg PA
CBHW082009230526
45468CB00023B/3008